W9-AVM-245

WORLD WAR II
JAPANESE AGGRESSION IN THE PACIFIC

WORLD WAR II

JAPANESE AGGRESSION IN THE PACIFIC

MASON CREST

Mason Crest
450 Parkway Drive, Suite D
Broomall, PA 19008
www.masoncrest.com

Printed and bound in the United States of America.

First printing
9 8 7 6 5 4 3 2 1

ISBN: 978-1-4222-3896-7
Series ISBN: 978-1-4222-3893-6
ebook ISBN: 978-1-4222-7906-9
ebook series ISBN: 978-1-4222-7903-8

Produced by Regency House Publishing Limited
The Manor House
High Street
Buntingford
Hertfordshire
SG9 9AB
United Kingdom

www.regencyhousepublishing.com

Text copyright © 2018 Regency House Publishing Limited/Christopher Chant.

PAGE 2: The battleship Pennsylvania, *largely undamaged, is seen behind the sunken destroyers* Downes *and* Cassin.

PAGE 3: *Pearl Harbor survivor Bill Johnson reads the list of names inscribed in the USS* Arizona *Memorial.*

RIGHT: *The deference paid to the emperor in Japan was total, confirmed here as the roadside crowd bows before the motorcade of the Emperor Hirohito.*

PAGE 6: USS Yorktown *in Pearl Harbor.*

CONTENTS

KEY ICONS TO LOOK FOR:

 Words to Understand: These words with their easy-to-understand definitions will increase the reader's understanding of the text, while building vocabulary skills.

 Sidebars: This boxed material within the main text allows readers to build knowledge, gain insights, explore possibilities, and broaden their perspectives by weaving together additional information to provide realistic and holistic perspectives.

 Educational Videos: Readers can view videos by scanning our QR codes, providing them with additional content to supplement the text. Examples include news coverage, moments in history, speeches, iconic sports moments, and much more!

 Text-Dependent Questions: These questions send the reader back to the text for more careful attention to the evidence presented here.

 Research Projects: Readers are pointed toward areas of further inquiry connected to each chapter. Suggestions are provided for projects that encourage deeper research and analysis.

 Series Glossary of Key Terms: This back-of-the-book glossary contains terminology used throughout the series. Words found here increase the reader's ability to read and comprehend high-level books and articles in this field.

OPPOSITE: *President Franklin D. Roosevelt signing the declaration of war against Japan, in the wake of the attack on Pearl Harbor.*

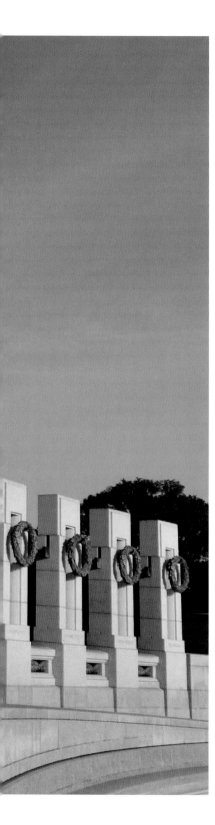

National World War II Memorial

The National World War II Memorial in Washington, D.C., is dedicated to the 16 million people who served in the American armed forces during World War II. The memorial also honors the 400,000 who gave the ultimate sacrifice for their country. Those who supported the war effort at home are honored too. The memorial symbolizes World War II as the defining event of the 20th century.

The memorial is situated on a 7.4-acre (3-hectare) site. It was created by designer and architect Friedrich St. Florian who won a national open competition for its design. The construction of memorial took place between 2001 and 2004 and then opened to the public on April 29, 2004; its official dedication took place a month later, on May 29. It was commission by President Clinton in 1993 who authorized the American Battle Monuments Commission (ABMC) to establish a World War II memorial in the Washington, D.C. area.

The memorial is an elliptical shaped plaza built around a splendid fountain and pool, with water jets in its center. Built in a semi-classical style, there are 56 granite columns forming a semi-circle around the perimeter. Each one is designed to symbolize the unity of the states, federal territories, and District of Columbia. The entry walkway is flanked by ornate balustrades decorated with 24 bronze bas-reliefs.

At the mid point of the plaza there are two pavillions decorated with bronzes, featuring Baldachins, American Eagles, and World War II Victory Medals. The pavillions represent the Atlantic and Pacific theaters.

At the western end of the memorial is a curved Freedom Wall bearing a field of 4,048 golden stars, each of which stands for 100 American military deaths in the war. Before it lies a granite curb inscribed "Here we mark the price of freedom."

Throughout the memorial are inscribed quotations from eminent military and political figures, including Gen. (later Pres.) Dwight D. Eisenhower, U.S. Presidents Franklin D. Roosevelt and Harry S. Truman, Col. Oveta Culp Hobby, Adm. Chester W. Nimitz, Gen. George C. Marshall, and Gen. Douglas MacArthur.

The National World War II Memorial is located at the east end of the Reflecting Pool on the Mall, opposite the Lincoln Memorial and west of the Washington Monument. The memorial is maintained by the U.S. National Park Service, and receives almost 5 million visitors each year. It is open 24 hours a day and is free to all visitors.

WORLD WAR II
Chapter One
PEARL HARBOR

On July 26, 1941 the government of the USA froze all Japanese assets in the country, a measure that was soon also implemented by the British government and the Dutch government in exile. This triple blow to Japan's position as a trading nation resulted from the Japanese empire's continued expansion on the mainland of Asia: ever since the beginning of the 2nd Sino-Japanese War in 1937 the

Words to Understand

Medievalism: Beliefs and customs of the Middle Ages.

Neutralize: To counteract activity or make ineffective.

Surrender: To yield to the power or control of another.

USA and UK had become increasingly concerned about the growth of Japanese military domination in eastern Asia. Various measures analogous to the freezing of Japanese assets had previously been tried, but Japan had taken little notice until this new move, inspired by the

Japanese occupation of French Indochina, starting on September 22, 1940. The threat implicit in the U.S. move of July 26 was reinforced on August 17 when President Franklin D. Roosevelt warned the government of Japan that any further Japanese efforts

to secure a paramount position in eastern Asia would serve to elicit U.S. retaliation to safeguard its policies and financial interests. While these overt moves were setting the scene for what was to follow, it should be noted that American-Japanese negotiations

OPPOSITE: The U.S. Pacific Fleet, seen here in 1940, was the primary offensive and defensive weapon available to the USA in the Pacific theater. It was therefore one of the primary targets selected by the Japanese for neutralization in the first minutes of its war of aggression into the Pacific and South-East Asia.

ABOVE: As well as the ships and aircraft of the U.S. Pacific fleet, the Japanese attack on the Hawaiian Islands targeted the aircraft of the U.S. Army Air Forces, such as this Curtiss P-40 fighter, lying badly damaged on the ground.

RIGHT: The newspaper headlines tell it all: as part of their grand offensive in December 1941, the Japanese launched a series of carefully planned land offensives under the cover of potent air power.

on the means of reducing tension between the two countries were being held in Washington, DC.

The reason why the USA, in particular, was taking these steps against Japan was basically a conflict of interest. Since the Spanish-American War of 1898–99, the Americans had been well placed in the Philippines and other Pacific island groups, inherited from the Spanish, to play a dominant role in Chinese economic affairs. This, combined with the emergence of China from its ancient monarchism into the type of democracy acceptable to the U.S. people, meant that in the USA China had a powerful friend. Japan, too, had only latterly emerged from its self-imposed **medievalism**. But unlike China, Japan had kept its ancient institutions, while at the same time managing to develop itself rapidly into a modern industrial nation with distinct military leanings. These military ambitions had been exercised at the expense of China in 1894–95, Imperial Russia in 1904–05, and Imperial Germany in 1914. Japan's major problem, however, lay in the fact that although it had turned itself into a major manufacturing nation with great energy, the Japanese empire had neither sufficient raw materials to feed its industries, nor the markets to support them. Raw materials could be obtained from all over eastern Asia, and there was a huge market in China. Hence Japan's interest in securing a political and economic hegemony over the major economic bases in this area, such as Manchuria, China, South-East Asia, and the British and Dutch East Indies. Its swift advance into the first of these areas inevitably brought Japan into conflict with the western democracies, which also had considerable economic interests in these countries.

By the 1930s, therefore, different political and economic interests had already set Japan and the western powers apart. These differences, crystallized as Japan took over Manchuria, started a war with China, with Japan then turning its attention south to Indochina and the Dutch East Indies. The USA's feelings in the matter were already plain in its supply of arms to China, via the Burma Road from Lashio, in northern Burma, to Chunking in China, and Roosevelt's two moves, mentioned above, finally made the U.S. position entirely clear. But Japan could not survive without raw materials and a market, and it also needed the oil that was so plentiful in the Indies. Thus the freezing of Japanese assets by the western powers did nothing to resolve the underlying problem: Japan's

OPPOSITE: *Photograph taken from a Japanese plane during the torpedo attack on ships moored on both sides of Ford Island shortly after the beginning of the Pearl Harbor attack. View looks about east, with the supply depot, submarine base, and fuel tank farm in the right center distance.*

A torpedo has just hit USS West Virginia on the far side of Ford Island (center). Other battleships moored nearby are (from left): Nevada, Arizona, Tennessee (inboard of West Virginia), Oklahoma (torpedoed and listing) alongside Maryland, and California.

On the near side of Ford Island, to the left, are light cruisers Detroit and Raleigh, target and training ship Utah and seaplane tender Tangier. Raleigh and Utah have been torpedoed, and Utah is listing sharply to port.

Japanese planes are visible in the right center (over Ford Island) and over the Navy Yard at right. U.S. Navy planes on the seaplane ramp are on fire.

海軍省許可済第七八二

teeming population needed to live, and western interests were getting in the way.

Poor as the situation was during September 1941, it became immeasurably worse on October 17, 1941 when Lieutenant-General Hideki Tojo became Japanese prime minister with the support of the nation's all-powerful military establishment. While not discounting absolutely the negotiations going on in Washington, on November 5 Tojo revealed to his inner circle the plans for the war he felt was becoming increasingly certain.

By the end of November it had become clear that there could be no basis of understanding between Japan and the USA and, although negotiations continued, Japan now made the decision for war. Drawn up by staffs under the supervision of Field-Marshal Hajime Sugiyama, army chief of staff, and Admiral Osami Nagoya, navy chief of staff, the basic Japanese plan comprised three

ABOVE: *An Imperial Japanese Navy Mitsubishi A6M Zero fighter on the aircraft carrier Akagi.*

OPPOSITE: *U.S. troops man improvised field defenses on Oahu Island, in the Hawaiian group, for a more capable defense in the event of the Japanese launching another attack in the first days of the USA's involvement in World War II.*

sections, based on Japan's inability to wage a protracted war against industrial nations. Firstly, the Imperial Japanese navy was to **neutralize** the U.S. Pacific Fleet, the western powers' major striking force in the area, while the Imperial Japanese army and other elements of the navy seized the "Southern Resources Area" and adjacent territories necessary to defend it. Secondly, an impregnable defense perimeter was to be set up. Thirdly, any attempts to break through this perimeter were to be repulsed so decisively that the western powers would sue for peace on the basis of a *status quo*. The whole Japanese plan was based on the two-fold premise that its forces could so maul the western powers in the first stage of the war that Japan would

have the time to complete her defensive perimeter; and that the Japanese defense, based on the proven abilities of its forces, and operating on interior lines of communication, could not be breached by the westerners, operating of necessity over scanty lines of communication from main bases in the USA and Australia.

With the decision for war all but taken, steps to secure success in the first stage were set in hand. Here the aircraft-carriers of the Imperial Japanese navy were to play a decisive role in crippling the U.S. Pacific Fleet at its base, Pearl Harbor, in the Hawaiian Islands group. Comprising six aircraft carriers and supported by battleships, cruisers, submarines, and oilers, Vice-Admiral Chuichi Nagumo's 1st Air Fleet, otherwise

Attack on Pearl Harbour

known as the Striking Force, left the Kurile Islands on November 26, heading by a circuitous and little used route, and in total radio silence, toward a position north of the Hawaiian Islands. The Americans, who had broken the Japanese naval code, knew that Japan was finally

preparing for war, but expected that the first blow would fall on the Philippines or Malaya; decoded radio messages indicated that Japanese forces were massing in the vicinity of both of these major objectives. Several prewar exercises had taken an attack on Pearl Harbor into consideration, but all was peaceful there early on the morning of Sunday, December 7 1941.

Trainee radar operators on an inefficient set north of Pearl Harbor reported that many aircraft were heading toward the islands, but the base commander dismissed the report, thinking they were the Boeing B-17 Flying Fortress bombers expected at the time, and ordered the radar crews to stand down. What the radar operators had in fact seen was Nagumo's first strike of 190 aircraft, which was soon followed by another wave of 171. Surprise was complete, and the Japanese pilots found their targets neatly arranged in rows. The warplanes had a field day, allowing the Japanese to rack up a considerable score. This included eight battleships, of which three were sunk, one was capsized, and the remaining four seriously damaged; three cruisers and three destroyers sunk, as was a miscellany of smaller vessels; while on shore, 65 of the U.S. Army's 231 aircraft were destroyed, as were 196 belonging to the U.S. Navy, and 250 machines of the U.S. Marine Corps. Apart from these material losses, the Americans lost some 3,220 men dead

OPPOSITE: *The scene of devastation on December 7, 1941 on Ford Island, the U.S. naval air station and repair facility in the middle of Pearl Harbor. The two major failings of the Japanese attack were the escape of the U.S. Pacific Fleet's three aircraft carriers, which were temporarily absent from Pearl Harbor, and the decision not to make another attack for the destruction of Pearl Harbor's repair facilities and fuel farms*

ABOVE: *The "Brooklyn"-class cruiser* Phoenix *escaped damage in the Japanese attack on Pearl Harbor. It is seen here steaming out of the anchorage, past clouds of heavy smoke from less fortunate U.S. Navy vessels and installations. The ship survived World War II and was sold to Argentina in 1951. Aircraft carriers and cruisers constituted the U.S. Navy's most important Pacific assets during the first half of 1942.*

and 1,272 wounded, as opposed to the Japanese losses which were slight.

The blow to American strength and pride was enormous. The claim often made that Japan did not declare war before the attack on Pearl Harbor is true but not completely so. Japan did try to declare war, but its embassy staff in Washington were so slow in decoding the relevant message that the attack had begun before the formal declaration could be made. U.S. intelligence, however, had decoded the message in good time, but the news was not sent out quickly enough to allow the U.S. defenses to be brought onto a war footing. Nevertheless,

Japan had now entered the war, turning what had previously been a European conflict into a global one.

The only solace the U.S. Navy could find, on assessing the damage after Pearl Harbor, was the fact that the Pacific Fleet's three aircraft carriers, the *Enterprise*, *Lexington* and *Saratoga*, were absent and had therefore escaped damage, it being these ships that would take the war to Japan in the next few months. Despite the intense disappointment of the Imperial Japanese navy's airmen, that they had not been able to come to grips with their opposite numbers, the victory at Pearl Harbor was adjudged

a great one, fulfilling the needs of the first stage of the Japanese war plan.

Japan's other objective in this first stage of the conflict was the securing of the Southern Resources Area. Moves to this end were being made at the time of the Pearl Harbor attack, as were mopping-up operations against U.S. bases in the Pacific. Despite the fact that they had repulsed the first Japanese attack, with heavy losses on December 11, the gallant defenders of Wake Island were overwhelmed in a massive second attack on December 23, while at the foot of the Marianas Islands group, the tiny garrison of Guam had been swept aside on December 10.

These tiny U.S. islands, however, were very small fry compared with the Japanese objectives on the Asian mainland and the major island groups off its coast. On December 8 (to the west of the International Date Line, this day in Asia was the same as December 7 in areas to the east of the line, such as Hawaii) the Japanese 38th Division smashed through the mainland defenses of the British colony at Hong Kong, forcing Major-General C.M. Maltby's forces to fall back to the island. After a call for **surrender** had been refused, the Japanese assaulted the island on December 18, and by December 25 the small British garrison had been overrun.

Niihau Incident

The Japanese military had determined that some means was required for rescuing fliers whose aircraft were too badly damaged to return to their respective carriers. The island of Niihau, only 30 minutes flying time from Pearl Harbor, was designated as a suitable rescue point.

On December 7, 1941 the Zero flown by a 22 year old airman

Officer Shigenori Nishikaichi was damaged in the attack on Wheeler, so he flew to the rescue point on Niihau. The aircraft was further damaged on landing. Nishikaichi was helped from the wreckage by a native Hawaiian, named Hawila Kaleohano who, aware of the tension between the United States and Japan, took the pilot's maps and other documents. The island's residents lived in relative isolation so were completely unaware of the Japanese attack on Pearl Harbor. Nishikaichi enlisted the support of three Japanese-American residents in an attempt to recover the documents. During the ensuing struggles, Nishikaichi was killed and a Hawaiian civilian was wounded; one collaborator committed suicide, and his wife and the third collaborator were sent to prison. The Niihau incident, as it is now called, made headlines throughout the country.

OPPOSITE: *Pearl Harbor on October 30, 1941, looking southwest.*

ABOVE: *A destroyed Vindicator at Ewa field, the victim of one of the smaller attacks on the approach to Pearl Harbor*

Farther south, the three divisions of Lieutenant-General Tomoyuki Yamashita's 25th Army had landed at Khota Bharu in northern Malaya and at Singora and Patani just over the border in Thailand on December 8. The British command in Malaya was in turmoil, and the troops at the front were poorly trained; thus, after the small RAF strength in the area had been overwhelmed by superior Japanese air power, Yamashita's 100,000 men were able to move smoothly inland toward the ultimate object of any invasion of Malaya, the great island fortress of Singapore. The Japanese split into two main lines of advance, one on each side of the Malayan peninsula, and moved swiftly south. The British commander, Lieutenant-General A.E. Percival, had some 100,000 men under his command, in three divisions, but had expected the Japanese landings to be made farther south. He now tried desperately to regroup his forces to meet the actual threat, but failed to do more than slow the Japanese

marginally. Right from the beginning of the campaign, the Japanese had displayed the considerable offensive tactical skill that was to make them so feared in the first two years of the war: operating on light scales of equipment, and without masses of motorized transport, their forward elements were able to slip around through the jungle flanks of British defensive positions and establish roadblocks in their rear. Cut off, the British forces did not have the tactical skills to escape through the jungle, and so had to surrender. Thus the Japanese moved swiftly south, leapfrogging the British defensive positions to keep up the momentum

of their offensive. As 1941 ended, the British found themselves being driven steadily to the south.

Soon after the shock of the first landings, the British had been further discomforted by the loss of their only two capital ships in the area. On hearing of the Japanese landings, Admiral Sir Tom Phillips had raced north from Singapore with the battleship *Prince of Wales* and the battle-cruiser *Repulse*, to engage the Japanese forces supporting the landings. The RAF could not provide air support, and on December 10, unable to find the Japanese, Phillips turned south. Japanese air strikes found him, and after a furious battle

the two British capital ships succumbed to large numbers of bomb and torpedo hits.

Meanwhile the Japanese had also landed in the Philippines, the 50,000 men of Lieutenant-General Masaharu Homma's 14th Army starting to come ashore on Luzon during December 10. The defense of this client nation of the USA rested on the 130,000 men of General Douglas MacArthur's U.S. and Filipino forces, of which only 22,400 were fully trained. Most of the U.S. Asiatic Fleet was withdrawn to Java, but the air forces in the Philippines, under the command of Major-General Lewis H. Brereton, were expected to administer a rude shock to the Japanese. Quite the contrary took place: an attack on December 8 caught the U.S. air forces lined up neatly on their airfields. Eighteen of the 35 B-17 bombers and 56 fighters were destroyed, as well as a number of other machines. This was particularly shaming for the Americans, since they had received ample warning of Japan's entry into the war. With the destruction of these aircraft, the USA lost their only adequate striking force.

MacArthur's defense plans were based on the likelihood of the Japanese landing at Lingayen Gulf and driving on to Manila, so he had disposed his forces in two main

Isoroku Yamamoto (1884–1943)
Yamamoto was a Japanese naval officer and commander-in-chief of the Combined Fleet during World War II until his death in the Solomon Islands.

After graduating from the Japanese Naval Academy in 1904 Yamamoto held several important posts in the Imperial Japanese Navy, and was responsible for many of its reorganizations and management. He was the commander-in-chief during the decisive early years of the Pacific War and so was responsible for major battles such as Pearl Harbor and Midway. U.S. forces finally managed to catch up with Yamamoto when his plane was shot down over Bougainville Island in 1943.

OPPOSITE: *Other victims of the attack on Pearl Harbor were the battleships Oklahoma, Maryland and West Virginia. The West Virginia was hit by seven torpedoes, the seventh tearing away her rudder; the Oklahoma was hit by four torpedoes, the last two above her belt armor, capsizing her; and the Maryland was hit by two 16-inch (406-mm) naval shells converted into armor-piercing bombs, neither of which caused serious damage.*

groupings to the north and south of the capital. But between December 10 and 20, Homma landed his forces to the north and south of Luzon, where they were able to consolidate and build airfields unmolested by the Americans. Then between December 20 and the end of the year, further landings were made to secure the islands of Mindanao and Jolo, where more airfields were built. Finally, the force for the main Japanese landings on Luzon arrived in Lingayen Gulf on December 22. The Japanese came ashore without opposition and soon moved south, the bulk of the Filipino army having been saved only by the resolution of the U.S. forces and the Philippine Scouts.

Another landing was made south of Manila in Limon Bay on December 24 and MacArthur, with his forces caught between the arms of an effective pincer, had to abandon his plan for a counterattack and withdraw

toward the last-ditch defensive position in the Bataan peninsula north-west of Manila. Here, he expected to hold out until reinforcements were brought in by the Pacific Fleet. Although MacArthur was often criticized for allowing his forces to be bottled up in this way, his withdrawal was in fact the right move. The Japanese, who had allocated only 50 days for the conquest of the Philippines, expected MacArthur to defend Manila, where the better Japanese troops could have made mincemeat of the U.S. and Filipino forces. But MacArthur's retreat to Bataan frustrated this expectation, considerably delaying the Japanese plans to take the Southern Resources Area.

Back in Malaya, the start of 1942 found the British in poor shape. Pushed steadily back, their final defense line on the mainland was breached on January 15, and by the

end of the month only the island fortress of Singapore was left. The fortress had been designed solely against attack from the sea, whereas the Japanese were now attacking from the landward side, where there were no fixed defenses or heavy artillery. On February 8 the Japanese landed on the island, and after desperate fighting captured the water reservoirs. This sealed the fate of the population and garrison, which surrendered unconditionally on February 15, with some 70,000 British troops being taken prisoner. The disaster was total, being the result mainly of poor planning and parsimony before the war. In the short term, it put the Japanese in a fine position for their planned invasion of the rich Dutch East Indies.

The new year also brought further success to the Japanese in the Philippines, albeit at great cost and delay to the overall plan. Two major assaults, in the middle and end of January, were beaten off by MacArthur's forces, but overcrowding and disease were rapidly eroding the Americans' ability to survive. Ordered to escape to Australia, MacArthur handed over command to Lieutenant-General Jonathan Wainwright on March 11, during a period when the Japanese were waging a war of attrition. On April 3, Homma, his forces now reinforced and rested, was able to launch the decisive offensive,

and as the defense forces began to crumble the Americans surrendered Bataan on April 9. At about the same time, Japanese forces were mopping up on the other islands, on which the defense had dissolved to form nuclei of guerrilla forces; now only the fortress island of Corregidor in

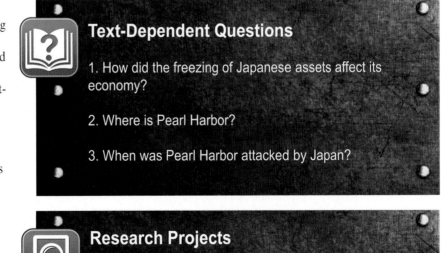

Text-Dependent Questions

1. How did the freezing of Japanese assets affect its economy?

2. Where is Pearl Harbor?

3. When was Pearl Harbor attacked by Japan?

Research Projects

What is the history behind the Japanese attack on Pearl Harbor?

OPPOSITE *The battleship* Pennsylvania, *largely undamaged, is seen behind the sunken destroyers* Downes *and* Cassin.

ABOVE RIGHT: *Captain Homer N. Wallin (center) supervises salvage operations aboard USS California, early 1942*

Manila Bay remained to deny the Japanese the use of Manila harbor. After an intense bombardment, the Japanese landed on May 5, and after savage fighting secured this final American position in the Philippines on the following day.

The skill of Japan's fighting forces is borne out by the relative losses in these campaigns: in Malaya 138,700 British against 9,820 Japanese, and in the Philippines 140,000 U.S. and Filipino against some 12,000 Japanese. Most of the Allied losses, however, were made up of prisoners or deserters from the Filipino army.

LEFT: *Japanese troops search a British prisoner.*

BELOW: *A victory parade in Tokyo. In the first nine months of the war, the Japanese armies were able to sweep all before them.*

OPPOSITE: *The deference paid to the emperor in Japan was total, confirmed here as the roadside crowd bows before the motorcade of the Emperor Hirohito.*

WORLD WAR II
Chapter Two
THE JAPANESE PRESS ON

By the end of 1941 the Japanese were effectively masters of the Malay **peninsula** and the Philippines, the remaining Allied forces in the areas being bottled up and incapable of taking any initiative. Yet Malaya and the Philippines were only half of the Southern Resources Area, the other two being the Indies, both Dutch and British, and Burma. The Indies offered rich pickings in oil, rubber and other raw materials, while Burma had oil, **tungsten**, and rubber. In addition, the Japanese saw that the seizure of Burma would cut the Burma Road to China, and thus sever their longest-standing adversary's sole remaining lifeline to the rest of the world. Both Malaya and the Philippines offered excellent jumping-off points for the East Indies

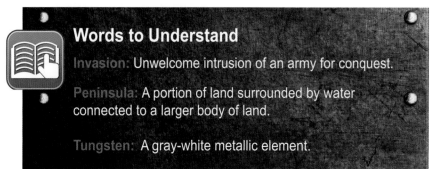

Words to Understand

Invasion: Unwelcome intrusion of an army for conquest.

Peninsula: A portion of land surrounded by water connected to a larger body of land.

Tungsten: A gray-white metallic element.

campaign, and similar advantages for the Burma operation were secured by the quiet occupation of Thailand, this also providing an overland line of communication with the forces in Malaya.

The British plan for the defense of Burma had been bedevilled by lack of resources, optimism that it would not be attacked, and divided

command. Thus, Lieutenant-General Thomas Hutton had only two under-strength divisions, with totally inadequate reserves and logistical backing with which to oppose the advance of the two strong divisions of Lieutenant-General Shojiro Iida's 15th Army. These heavily supported and reinforced divisions attacked

LEFT: The Japanese were not great advocates of armored warfare, for they lacked the industrial power and materials for the mass-production of tanks, and most of the terrain over which their armies fought their campaigns was little suited to armored warfare. This is a Type 89B medium tank, armed with one 2.24-inch (57-mm) main gun and two machine guns.

OPPOSITE ABOVE: Japanese infantry in the Philippines. Fast, tough, resilient, and able to prosper on modest quantities of indifferent food, the Japanese soldier soon disproved the western myth that he was a poor fighting man.

OPPOSITE BELOW: Manila, the capital of the Philippine Islands, was protected by U.S. forts in and around Manila Bay. The Japanese took Manila from the landward side, and the exposed guns of the forts, such as this 12-inch (305-mm) weapon on Corregidor, proved vulnerable to air attack and largely irrelevant to the campaign.

from Thailand toward Moulmein and
Tavoy, in the long, thin "tail" of
Burma, on January 12, 1942. Hutton's
forces were soon in difficulty, and had
to start withdrawing behind the
Salween river line by the end of
January. Pressing on quickly, the 15th
Army outflanked the British by
crossing the Salween upstream,
forcing Hutton's tired troops to pull
back once again, this time toward the
Sittang river. Once again the Japanese
had outflanked the British by crossing
the Sittang first, and part of the 17th
Indian Division was lost when the
only bridge over the Sittang was
blown up on February 23. Realizing
that matters were becoming desperate,
the British appointed Lieutenant-
General Sir Harold Alexander to
command, with orders to hold
Rangoon. Reinforcements brought
British strength back up to some two
very under-strength divisions, which
Alexander appreciated could not
hope to hold Rangoon. The British
forces therefore prepared to retreat
up the Irrawaddy and Sittang rivers,
with Alexander only just escaping
capture as the Japanese took
Rangoon on March 7, two days after
he had taken command.

Although the situation looked
hopeless, as Rangoon had been the
only major means of surface
communication with India, things
looked up momentarily with the
arrival of the first Chinese troops in
the area. These had been offered by
Chiang Kai-shek, the Chinese
generalissimo, when he realized that
his lifeline to the western world was
being threatened. The Chinese 5th and
6th Armies, each the equivalent of a
strong British division, were under the
command of Lieutenant-General
Joseph "Vinegar Joe" W. Stilwell,

Chiang's US chief of staff. During March 13–20 a defense line was established between Prome on the Irrawaddy and Toungoo on the Sittang, the British holding the former and the Chinese the latter. During this period, Major-General William Slim arrived to assume command of the British "Burcorps." By the end of the month, however, the Japanese had driven back the Chinese, forcing the British to retreat to avoid being outflanked. The same thing happened again at Yenangyaung, the location of Burma's main oilfields, during April 10–19, although this time it was the British who were forced to fall back in the face of Japanese pressure.

As this battle continued, the Japanese also launched an offensive against the Chinese 6th Army in the area between the Sittang and Salween rivers in the Loikaw and Taunggyi area, and by April 23 the Chinese army had disintegrated, causing the remaining Chinese and the British to fall back, again to prevent being outflanked. But the Japanese 56th Division rushed north, filling the vacuum left by the Chinese 6th Army to seize Lashio on the Burma Road. The Japanese, now three divisions strong, were thus well placed to cut the Allied line of retreat, and headed

ABOVE LEFT: *Japanese troops move through the railroad yards at Johor Bahru.*

LEFT: *A Japanese mortar battery in China.*

OPPOSITE ABOVE: *The U.S. and Filipino forces' last major bastion area in the Philippines was the Bataan peninsula. Here a U.S. soldier catches a brief moment of rest.*

OPPOSITE BELOW: *Japanese troops on the move in Thailand, which was an ally of Japan in World War II and in effect under Japanese control.*

south-west toward Mandalay to do just this. However, the Allies managed to fall back through this city just before the Japanese arrived on May 1.

The Allies now split up in order to make their final escape. The British managed to fight their way north-west to Kalewa and thence over appalling mountains to the Manipur plain and India, while the remnants of Stilwell's Chinese forces continued north, some branching off toward Yunnan in China, the rest going with Stilwell north-east to safety at Ledo in northern Assam.

The Japanese were the masters of Burma by the end of May 1942, and China's supply route from the west had been severed. Some 30,000 of the 42,000 British troops involved in the campaign had been lost, together with large numbers of the 95,000 Chinese involved, compared with Japanese casualties of a mere 7,000 men. As the Japanese consolidated, Stilwell set about retraining his Chinese, while the British attempted to set their house in order to resist any Japanese invasion of India and to prepare the forces for a reconquest of Burma. Deprived of their land communications with China, the Americans had recourse to the expensive and difficult means of flying supplies over the Himalayas from India as engineers set about building a new road to China from Ledo.

Meanwhile, the Japanese had been building on their successes in the southern area. Supported by the carriers of Vice-Admiral Chuichi Nagumo's 1st Air Fleet, three Japanese amphibious forces invaded the East Indies. After landings to secure bases in Borneo and Celebes in early January, the main operations gained momentum. The Eastern Force

moved via Sulawesi, the Moluccas and Timor toward Bali and Java; the Center Force advanced via the Macassar Strait and the east coast of Borneo toward Java; and the Western Force moved via the South China Sea and northern Borneo toward Sumatra. Each of these forces had powerful cruiser escorts for the troopships carrying the men of the Japanese 16th Army, and support from land-based aircraft as well as Nagumo's carriers. Under the command of General Sir Archibald Wavell's American British Dutch Australian Command (ABDACOM), the mixed Allied forces could offer no real resistance, and the Japanese moved swiftly south. ABDACOM was dissolved on February 25, and the forces in the islands were left to fight on under Dutch command. With a few notable exceptions, Allied naval forces in the area came off worse in encounters with the Japanese naval task forces, and the fate of the Dutch East Indies was sealed with the decisive defeat of the Dutch Rear-Admiral Karel Doorman's force of five cruisers and ten destroyers by Rear-Admiral Takeo

ABOVE The U.S. survivors after the surrender of Bataan on April 9, 1942 were then subjected to the brutal "Bataan death march" to their prisoner of war camps.

OPPOSITE ABOVE: Japanese 12th Army men cross a river in China on an improvised ferry.

OPPOSITE RIGHT: Japanese light tanks ford a shallow river near Nanking in China. Lacking the manpower to take and hold the whole of China, the Japanese concentrated their efforts on the eastern part of the country, adjacent to the East China Sea, and other areas rich in resources.

northern coast of New Guinea and in the Bismarck archipelago. On March 13 they also landed on Bougainville, northernmost of the major islands in the Solomon chain.

The U.S. carrier forces were not idle during this period, however. Attacks had been launched on the Gilbert and the Marshall Islands groups on February 1, on Rabaul on February 20, Wake Island four days later, Marcus Island on March 4 and on Lae and Salamaua on March 10. Finally, on April 18, 16 USAAF North American B-25 Mitchell twin-engined bombers were flown off the carrier *Hornet* to make a nuisance raid on Tokyo. This had an important effect on the Japanese morale, and also, despite the Allied setbacks, in Australia, where General Douglas MacArthur was readying land forces for the counteroffensive. At Pearl Harbor, moreover, the U.S. Navy was preparing plans for an offensive across the Pacific.

In the Indian Ocean, the Imperial Japanese navy had also been making itself felt with the arrival of Nagumo's 1st Air Fleet, its five carriers supported by four battleships. During April 2–8, Nagumo's warplanes struck at Trincomalee and Colombo in Ceylon, and also sank one aircraft carrier, two cruisers and one destroyer of the British Eastern Fleet before retiring back into the Pacific. Worried by the threat of further Japanese ambitions in the Indian Ocean and even Africa, the British seized the Vichy French island of Madagascar between May and November 1942. In fact, the tide of the Japanese expansion had by now reached full flood.

Takagi's four cruisers and 13 destroyers in the Battle of the Java Sea on February 27, the allies losing two cruisers and five destroyers. The obsolete aircraft deployed by the Allies in the theater had already been knocked out, and with the losses of the Java Sea battle were soon augmented as the Allied warships were picked off, leaving the Japanese in control.

Between February 29 and March 9, when the Dutch East Indies finally capitulated, they made swift progress. At the same time, other Japanese forces had secured bases along the

In an essentially impossible effort to tackle Japanese troop convoys off north-eastern Malaya, the new battleship Prince of Wales *(seen here leaving Singapore)* and the old battle-cruiser Repulse *were subjected to a devastating Japanese land-based air attack, both ships being sunk in less than an hour.*

OPPOSITE: *Although difficult to assess, as thousands of captives were able to escape from their guards along the way, about 54,000 of the 72,000 prisoners on the Bataan death march reached their destination, with approximately 5,000–10,000 Filipino and 600–650 U.S. prisoners of war dying on their journey to Camp O'Donnell.*

OVERLEAF: *Aerial view of USS Arizona and USS Missouri Memorials at Ford Island, Pearl Harbor, Honolulu, Hawaii, USA.*

Text-Dependent Questions

1. What valuable natural resources did Burma have?

2. When did the Japanese capture Rangoon?

3. When did the Dutch East Indies finally capitulate?

Research Projects

What sparked Japan's aggression in World War II?

WORLD WAR II

Chapter Three
THE TIDE TURNS: THE BATTLES OF THE CORAL SEA AND MIDWAY

Many disasters followed in the train of Pearl Harbor: the fall of Malaya, the East Indies, and the destruction of Allied naval strength in the Battle of the Java Sea. The precarious Allied command structure, set up in December 1941, was in ruins, and the first requirement for the Allies was to find new, secure bases from which to plan the destruction of the Japanese.

Words to Understand

Dive-bomber: An airplane that makes a steep dive to its target before releasing a bomb.

Fleet: A number of warships under a single command.

Theory: An analysis of a set of facts in relation to one another.

OPPOSITE: *The fleet carrier* Lexington, *seen on fire before sinking in the Battle of the Coral Sea. The battle was a slight Japanese victory at the tactical level, but in strategic terms was a U.S. success as the Japanese were forced to call off their effort to make an amphibious assault on Port Moresby in southern Papua.*

ABOVE: *One of the warplanes that helped to check the tide of Japanese success was the Douglas SBD Dauntless two-seat dive-bomber. Small and sturdy, the Dauntless could deliver its weapon with great accuracy. Here, the aircraft are waiting to take off from the fleet carrier* Yorktown, *early in 1942.*

RIGHT: *The Japanese fleet carrier* Shokaku *under air attack in the Battle of the Coral Sea. This was the world's first naval battle in which the surface combatants did not come within sight of each other.*

The war theater was vast, stretching from New Zealand to the Aleutian Islands Group, but by April 1942 General Douglas MacArthur had taken over as Supreme Allied Commander, South-West Pacific, and his naval opposite number, Admiral Chester Nimitz, as Commander-in-Chief, Pacific. The Japanese, of course, did not wait for the Allied forces to regain their balance, and on April 20 a Japanese invasion force left Truk in the Caroline Islands for the Solomon Islands and New Guinea. The Japanese would then find it easy to attack Australia, the cornerstone of Allied power in the south-west Pacific, from bases to be captured there.

Nimitz was alerted to the Japanese intentions by the same team of cryptanalysts whose warning of the Pearl Harbor attack had been ignored. He wasted no time in sending two aircraft carriers, the *Yorktown* and *Lexington*, under Rear-Admiral Frank Jack Fletcher, to the new extemporized base at Espiritu Santo. Against these the Japanese mustered

OPPOSITE ABOVE: *The United States Navy fleet oiler USS* Neosho *(AO-23) is left burning and slowly sinking after an attack by Imperial Japanese Navy dive bombers on May 7, 1942 during the Battle of the Coral Sea.*

OPPOSITE BELOW: *A view of aircraft carrier USS* Lexington *exploding on May 8, 1942, several hours after being damaged by a Japanese carrier air attack.*

ABOVE: *Shigeyoshi Inoue, commander of the 4th Fleet of the Imperial Japan Navy.*

RIGHT: *Admiral Frank Jack Fletcher, commander of U.S. Task Force 17.*

two fleet carriers, the *Shokaku* and *Zuikaku*, the light carrier *Shoho* and the seaplane carrier *Kamikawa Maru*. Battle was joined on May 3 when the Japanese landed on Tulagi in the Solomons. The Americans soon launched attacks on the invasion force, and these inflicted considerable damage. Both carrier task forces maneuvered for two days without making contact, but at first light on May 7 reconnaissance aircraft sent

back their sighting reports and an air attack was launched by each side. The first U.S. attack on the *Shoho* did no damage, but the *Yorktown*'s aircraft were able to inflict heavy damage shortly after this. Within 10 minutes of the first torpedo hit, the *Shoho* was sinking.

The Japanese had no such success, for their aircraft erroneously sank a fleet oiler and a destroyer under the impression they were a

carrier and a light cruiser. A later attack, looking for the *Yorktown*, was mauled by the U.S. carrier's combat air patrol and lost nine aircraft. When a group of Japanese aircraft mistook the *Yorktown* for a friendly ship, gunfire accounted for a further 11 aircraft, making a loss of 17 percent

The Battle of Midway

of the Japanese carriers' strength without a proper attack having been launched against either the *Lexington* or *Yorktown*.

On the following day, the U.S. carrierborne warplanes attacked again, managing to damage the *Shokaku* with two bomb hits, but further attacks were not successful. This time the Japanese pilots were able to strike back, catching the *Lexington* and *Yorktown* together at about an hour before noon. The nimble *Yorktown* was hit by only one bomb and managed to contain the fire which broke out, but the older *Lexington* was hit by two torpedoes and two bombs. The fire was much more serious and about an hour later the ship suffered a severe internal fuel explosion. The vessel continued to blaze and was finally abandoned four hours later, sinking three hours after that.

The U.S. Navy was bitterly disappointed by the outcome of this, the Battle of the Coral Sea, but the Americans' tactical defeat was small consolation for the Japanese, in that they were forced to cancel the amphibious landing planned for Port Moresby, in favor of an overwhelmingly difficult overland advance. As important in the long run was the damage to *Shokaku* and the depletion of the two surviving carrier air groups, which meant that both were unable to take part in the decisive Battle of Midway. The Battle of the Coral Sea had robbed the Japanese of an objective for the first time, and ultimately made certain an

ABOVE: *The Japanese fleet carrier Shokaku under air attack in the Battle of the Coral Sea. This was the world's first naval battle in which the surface combatants did not come within sight of each other.*

The U.S. fleet carrier, Yorktown, was severely damaged in the Battle of the Coral Sea, but was then repaired with almost incredible speed to play a major role in the Battle of Midway, in which the ship suffered more major damage. Taken in tow, the aircraft carrier was finally torpedoed and sunk by a Japanese submarine.

eventual Allied victory in the south-west Pacific.

The Japanese were troubled by their failure to secure New Guinea, which did not stop them from pursuing their other objectives in the north and central Pacific. The grand strategic aim had always been to force the Americans into a main fleet action, and although Pearl Harbor had eliminated virtually all of the U.S. Pacific Fleet's battleships, its aircraft carriers were still at large. Realizing that Nimitz was far too wily to fritter away his strength attacking the Japanese homeland, the commander-in-chief of the 1st Fleet, Admiral Isoroku Yamamoto, decided to lay a more subtle trap. If he occupied Midway Island, at the extreme north-western end of the Hawaiian Islands group, Yamamoto knew that the Americans would have

to fight him, this island being far too valuable as an outpost of the U.S. defensive perimeter to be allowed to fall into Japanese hands.

Yamamoto's plan called for an ambitious assault on Midway, backed by a powerful surface including four **fleet** carriers, while another force would simultaneously occupy the Aleutians, 1,500 miles (2400km) to the north. On paper, this was more than enough to crush the Americans, but had one major advantage in the fact that, once again, cryptanalysis had in good time revealed the broad outlines of the enemy deployment and Nimitz was able to plan his counterstroke in advance. Nevertheless, the Americans had so few ships that the margin between defeat and victory remained very narrow. Only two carriers were available, and they had to be brought from the south-west Pacific. The

Yorktown had been damaged in the Battle of the Coral Sea, but repairs had been made in an unbelievably short space of three days at Pearl Harbor. Although Yorktown had lost much of its air group, this was offset by survivors from the Lexington, and as a result the carrier could boast the most battle-hardened aircrew of all the U.S. carriers.

The Battle of the Coral Sea had shown that more fighters were needed, so 50 percent more Grumman F4F-4 Wildcat warplanes were embarked. The Douglas TBD Devastator torpedo-bomber had already proved most unsatisfactory, being too slow and with an ineffective torpedo, but there was no time to replace it with the new Grumman TBF-1 Avenger. The Japanese made no changes to their aircraft, which comprised the Mitsubishi A6M5 Reisen "Zero"

fighter, Aichi D3A "Val" **dive-bomber** and Nakajima B5N "Kate" torpedo-bomber, apart from embarking a pair of Yokosuka D4Y1 "Judy" fast reconnaissance aircraft in the carrier *Soryu* to improve the chances of sighting the U.S. fleet. Against the U.S. *Enterprise, Hornet,* and *Yorktown*, the Japanese could muster the carriers *Akagi, Kaga, Hiryu, Soryu,* and *Hosho*, and two seaplane

carriers. They had nine battleships, in addition, including the giant *Yamato* and 11 cruisers.

Forewarned of the true Japanese objectives, Fletcher, commanding at sea under Nimitz's overall supervision, was able to ignore the thrust toward the Aleutians. On June 2 Rear Admiral Raymond A. Spruance's Task Force 16 (*Enterprise* and *Hornet* with six cruisers and nine destroyers) and

ABOVE: *Armorers load bombs onto the underwing racks of a Consolidated PBY Catalina on Midway Island, an outpost to the north-west of the main part of the Hawaiian Islands and one of the primary targets for the Japanese in their complex Midway operation.*

OPPOSITE: *Midway Atoll. Aerial photograph, looking just south of west across the southern side of the atoll, November 24, 1941. Eastern Island, then the site of Midway's airfield, is in the foreground. Sand Island, location of most other base facilities, is across the entrance channel.*

Fletcher's TF 17 (*Yorktown* with two cruisers and five destroyers) were in position some 350 miles (560km) north of Midway. The invasion force was sighted on the following day, but Fletcher let shore-based aircraft from Midway attack it, still having no idea where Vice-Admiral Chuichi Nagumo's main carrier force might be

found. By nightfall on June 3 both carrier groups were approaching Midway, 460 miles (740km) apart and completely ignorant of each other's whereabouts. Midway, meanwhile, was under attack from Japanese bombers but held its own, leaving Fletcher and Spruance to concentrate on their main objective, the location and

destruction of the Japanese carriers.

By next morning, Nagumo's carriers were only 200 miles (320km) north-west of Midway, which was where the island's dawn patrol spotted them. Five minutes later TF 16 received orders to launch an attack, and soon 97 torpedo-bombers and dive-bombers were airborne.

Meanwhile, some 50 shore-based bombers had made an attack on Nagumo's carriers, without success, with a loss of 17 aircraft. Stung by this attack, Nagumo decided to reinforce the assault on Midway by throwing in the 93 aircraft he had retained in case of an attack from the U.S. carriers. The aircraft were sent down to the hangars for re-arming with bombs, just 14 minutes before Fletcher's task force was sighted. The report had omitted any mention of a carrier, so Nagumo's calculations still seemed to make sense. The Japanese admiral had been caught off balance, even if he did not fully realize the

ABOVE: Akagi, *the flagship of the Japanese carrier striking force which attacked Pearl Harbor.*

OPPOSITE: Devastators of VT-6 aboard USS Enterprise *being prepared for take off during battle.*

LEFT: *The Battle of Midway was a catastrophe of huge proportions for the Japanese, in that they lost four fleet carriers and most of their skilled aircrews, and in the process had the strategic initiative in the Pacific wrested from them by the Americans. This is the Hiryu, one of the four Japanese carriers to go down in flames before being scuttled. The other three were the Soryu, Kaga and Akagi, all four of which were veterans of the Pearl Harbor attack.*

BELOW: *Battle of Midway, June 1942. Burning oil tanks on Sand Island, Midway, following the Japanese air attack delivered on the morning of June 4, 1942. These tanks were located near what was then the southern shore of Sand Island. This view looks inland from the vicinity of the beach.*

OPPOSITE: *The crew or a U.S. Army Air Forces Martin B-26 Marauder, "Susie-Q") from the 18th Reconnaissance Squadron (Medium), 22nd Bomb Group, which made torpedo-attack on the Japanese carriers in the early morning of June 4, 1942 during the Battle of Midway. The plane had more than 500 bullet holes when it landed at Midway and was written off. The crew was allowed to cut out the nose-art "Susie-Q" before the plane was dumped at sea.*

fact. A series of unsuccessful attacks on his carriers by shore-based aircraft prevented Nagumo from recovering those machines which had been bombing Midway, with the result that many ran out of fuel. Nearly a third of the aircraft which had taken off were lost, but two hours after the first sighting report, Nagumo's carriers were finally ready to face TF 16 and TF 17.

The first attack by the *Hornet* and *Enterprise* was not coordinated with that launched by the *Yorktown*, and sustained heavy losses. But there were still 50 aircraft left from the *Enterprise* and *Yorktown*'s air groups, and these finally succeeded in crippling the *Akagi*, Nagumo's flagship, then in destroying the *Kaga* and *Soryu*. All three Japanese carriers succumbed quickly to devastating fires which swept through their hangars. The fourth carrier, the *Hiryu*, immediately launched a counterstrike, her aircraft flying straight to the *Yorktown* to hit her with three bombs. The U.S. carrier proved better able to cope with the fire, which inevitably followed, but was badly damaged and unable to recover its own fighters. Yet by heroic exertions the crew managed to get the ship under way again and even launched eight fighters to cope with a second attack from the *Hiryu*. This time, however, *Yorktown* was unable to dodge two torpedoes.

The last fight of the *Yorktown* had a decisive effect on the outcome

of the battle. The Japanese had assumed they were opposed by only two carriers, not knowing that the Pearl Harbor dockyard workers had achieved the impossible by repairing the *Yorktown*'s damage in only three days. Having hit one carrier badly, earlier in the day, the Japanese found it unbelievable that the same carrier

ABOVE: *Japanese prisoners of war on board USS Ballard (AVD-10) after being rescued from a lifeboat two weeks after the Battle of Midway. They were members of the aircraft carrier Hiryu's engineering force, left behind when she was abandoned on June 5, 1942, and had escaped in one of her boats just as she sank.*

LEFT: *Japanese heavy cruiser Mikuma, photographed from a USS Enterprise (CV-6) SBD aircraft during the Battle of Midway, after she had been bombed by planes from Enterprise and USS Hornet (CV-8). Note her shattered midships structure, torpedo dangling from the after port side tubes and wreckage atop her number four eight-inch gun turret.*

could be operational again in so short a time. Therefore the carrier which had just been sunk must have been the second carrier, making it safe to assume that both U.S. carriers had been knocked out. In fact there were still two undamaged ships. The *Enterprise* and *Hornet* had very few aircraft left, and only 40 bombers took off for a last desperate blow against the *Hiryu*. Their target was carrying about half the aircraft with which it had started, and although the Zero fighters were able to punish the attackers, they could not prevent the second wave from scoring four bomb hits. The ship started to burn, the fires slowly getting out of control. Incredibly, the other three carriers were still ablaze: the *Kaga* and *Soryu* did not sink until evening, and the *Akagi* lasted until dawn the following day. The *Hiryu* finally sank at 09.00am the next morning.

OPPOSITE: *USS Yorktown (CV-5) is hit on the port side, amidships, by a Japanese Type 91 aerial torpedo during the mid-afternoon attack by planes from the carrier Hiryu, in the Battle of Midway, on June 4, 1942. Yorktown is heeling to port and is seen at a different aspect than in other views taken by USS Pensacola (CA-24), indicating that this is the second of the two torpedo hits she received. Note very heavy antiaircraft fire.*

ABOVE: *USS* Yorktown *at Pearl Harbor days before the battle*

Yamamoto and his main body had been too far away to help, but he did realize that the plan had gone badly wrong. By ordering the three smaller carriers, *Zuiho, Ryujo,* and *Junyo,* south from the Aleutians he had hoped to concentrate a fresh force to trap the Americans in a night action. But Spruance, in command after the disabling of Fletcher's

Yorktown, wisely took TF 16 well clear to the east as soon as he had recovered the last aircraft. In **theory**, Yamamoto's four small carriers had mustered enough aircraft to defeat Spruance, but in practice the vast distances made it impossible to bring the ships together soon enough to score decisive hits. Yamamoto decided to bow to the inevitable, ordering his

invasion force to withdraw early on the morning of June 5.

This was the decisive moment of the Battle of Midway. The battle lasted for another two days, during which time other ships were sunk and a submarine put two more torpedoes into *Yorktown* to seal its fate. But these events were only a postscript. Midway marked the high tide of Japanese expansion in the Pacific, and although it did not appear obvious at the time, Japan had lost the strategic

initiative. Japanese aircrew casualties were much heavier than those of the USA. Much worse, the Japanese found it almost impossible to replace their highly-trained and combat-hardened veteran aircrews with men of anything like the same caliber. Nor could the shipyards turn out more carriers to replace the four sunk, whereas U.S. shipyards were already turning out fleet carriers in large numbers. Another nail in the Japanese coffin was the fact that, while they

could replace the aircraft they had lost, they could do so only with improved versions of the same types, which were approaching obsolescence; the Americans, on the other hand, were mass-producing vast numbers of a new generation of more advanced warplanes, to be flown by men progressing through a very thorough training program that involved instruction and guidance by veterans of the early battles. But the most important result of Midway was that

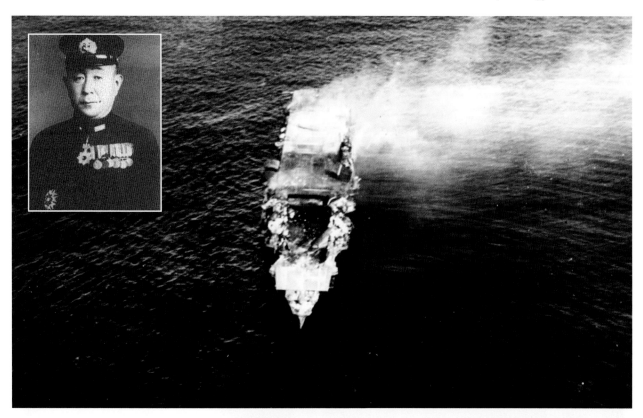

the Japanese had failed in their attempt to dislodge the Americans from their defensive perimeter. For Nimitz it was only a matter of waiting until the new ships were ready, before launching his drive across the central Pacific toward Japan.

ABOVE: *The U.S. Navy heavy cruiser USS Portland (CA-33), right, transfers survivors of the aircraft carrier USS Yorktown (CV-5) to the submarine tender USS Fulton (AS-11), left, on June 7, 1942, following the Battle of Midway.*

LEFT: *The Hiryu burning and sinking the morning after being bombed by U.S. aircraft during the Battle of Midway on June 4, 1942.*

INSET: *Japanese Vice Admiral Tamon Yamaguchi who went down with the Hiryu during the battle.*

Text-Dependent Questions

1. What was the Battle of Coral Sea?

2. What was the Battle of Midway?

3. Explain why the Japanese failed to dislodge the Americans from their defensive perimeter in the Battle of Midway?

Research Projects

Why did Japan never fully recover after the Battle of Midway?

WORLD WAR II

Chapter Four

THE ALLIES TAKE THE OFFENSIVE: NEW GUINEA AND GUADALCANAL

In May and June 1942, the Japanese decided to expand the defensive perimeter they were establishing to shield their newly-won possessions. This expansion was to take place primarily in the south-east, where Papua, the Bismarck, and the Solomon Islands were to be taken by the forces of Lieutenant-General Hitoshi Imamura's 8th Area Army.

Words to Understand

Fanatical: Excessive enthusiasm.

Guadalcanal: An island in the south-eastern Solomons.

Jungle: A tangled mass of tropical vegetation.

General Douglas MacArthur (1880–1964)
MacArthur was born on January 26, 1880 in Little Rock, Arkansas. One of America's greatest military leaders, he was a U.S. general who commanded the south-west Pacific Theater in World War II, where he was instrumental in defeating the Japanese. He was also involved in the administration and rebuilding of postwar Japan during the Allied occupation and served in the Korean War, leading the United Nations forces who ultimately prevented North Korean forces from overrunning South Korea.

OPPOSITE: *Supported by an M5 light tank, men of the U.S. Marine Corps land on Guadalcanal on August 7, 1942.*

ABOVE: *Australian infantrymen on the move in conditions typical of the fighting along the Kokoda Trail in Papua during the fall of 1942. Here the conditions and endemic diseases were as dangerous to them as the enemy.*

The keys to the territory, the Japanese decided, were Port Moresby on the southern coast of Papua, and the island of **Guadalcanal** in the Solomons. Major airfields in these two places would allow the Japanese to detect and destroy any Allied force attempting to break through the perimeter. Despite a first rebuff in the Battle of the Coral Sea, Imamura

pressed ahead with the plan, but now decided that the only way to take Port Moresby was by means of an overland advance from the north coast across the formidable Owen Stanley range, and from the east after a landing at Milne Bay. His first steps were

therefore to land troops at Gona, on the northern coast of Papua, on July 11, 1942, with another landing at nearby Buna shortly after this, then on Guadalcanal on July 6. The troops on Guadalcanal immediately set about building an airfield, while others in Papua began preparations for the advance toward Port Moresby.

The Americans were also trying to decide what they should do next.

General Douglas MacArthur, commanding the South-West Pacific Area, favored a direct thrust by the army on Rabaul, the town on New Britain where the Japanese had their theater headquarters, and Admiral Ernest J. King, the U.S. chief of naval operations, favored naval action in the Bismarck Islands and New Guinea area to disrupt the Japanese attack against the supply line across the

Pacific to Australia, combined with an island-hopping campaign toward Rabaul. The Joint Chiefs of Staff mediated between the commander of the South-West Pacific Area and the head of the U.S. Navy, and opted for a three-phase operation: the seizure of the southern Solomons by the forces of Vice-Admiral Robert L. Ghormley's South Pacific Area; the seizure of the rest of the Solomons by

MacArthur's forces; and finally the seizure of the north coast of New Guinea, New Britain and New Ireland, also by MacArthur's forces supported by the navy. Ghormley's forces were able to move quickly to their task, but MacArthur's first move was forestalled by the Japanese advance toward Port Moresby.

On July 21 the men of Major-General Tomitaro Horii's South Sea Detachment left their beach-head between Gona and Buna and moved off to the south-west. Local Australian forces could not halt the advancing Japanese, and pulled back before them into the Owen Stanley mountains, fighting desperate rearguard actions but failing to stop the skillful and determined Japanese advance along the Kokoda Trail. By August 12 the Japanese were over the crest of the mountains, and the exhausted Australians, starving and short of all essential supplies, were still falling back. As they approached Port Moresby, the Japanese too began to suffer from the effects of their nightmare crossing of the mountains, and were gradually being slowed by strengthening Australian and U.S. resistance under the command of an Australian officer, Lieutenant-General Edmund Herring. By September 26 the Japanese were halted at Ioribaiwa, only 30 miles (50km) from Port

OPPOSITE: The U.S. Navy aircraft carrier USS Enterprise (CV-6) seen from another U.S. ship while under attack by Japanese dive bombers during the Battle of the Eastern Solomons on August 24, 1942. An intense fire is burning in her starboard after five-inch gun gallery, the result of a bomb hit that ignited ready-service ammunition. Note the antiaircraft shell bursts over the carrier.

RIGHT: Lieutenant General Imamura Hitoshi.

Moresby. Three days earlier, the Australian 7th Division had started a counteroffensive, soon joined by the U.S. 32nd Division. Ordered by Imamura to fall back, Horii started his retreat at the end of the month, harried unmercifully by the Australian and U.S. forces. This time it was the Japanese who suffered the most terrible privations, especially shortages of food, and many died after trying to

eat grass and earth. By November 19 the Japanese were back where they had started in Buna and Gona.

Meanwhile, the other prong of the Japanese assault on Port Moresby had been defeated. On August 25 a regiment had landed at Milne Bay, but after serious fighting with the local forces had been wiped out. Port Moresby was now safe from overland assault.

Despite their losses and hardships, the Japanese were determined to hold Buna and Gona. Already the victims of the speed and aggression of Japanese offensive tactics, the Allies were now to be taught a desperate lesson in Japanese determination and skill in defense, especially from prepared positions. The Allied assault started on November 20, but at first made no progress whatsoever. Disease had decimated the Allied formations and morale was low. Matters were improved by the arrival of a new commander, Lieutenant-General Robert L. Eichelberger, on December 1, but it was not until December 7 that the Australians were able to batter their way into Gona against the shattered opposition. Buna still held out, the Australians and Americans

ABOVE: *A U.S. 11th Marines 75mm pack howitzer and crew on Guadalcanal, September or October, 1942. The lean condition of the crewmembers indicate that they haven't been getting enough nutrition during this period.*

OPPOSITE: *Lieutenant Colonel, later Colonel, Bill Whaling (lower left looking at map) photographed on Guadalcanal in August or September, 1942. Whaling led the Whaling Group of scouts and snipers during the Guadalcanal campaign.*

finally taking it against **fanatical** resistance on January 22, 1943. The Japanese had lost more than 7,000 dead and 350 prisoners taken, all wounded very badly. The Allies had lost 5,700 Australian and 2,783 American dead, with a further large number incapacitated by disease.

For the first time, the Japanese had been beaten on land, but they had shown how costly it would be for the Allies to win back all that they had lost. The Australians and Americans, on the other hand, had learned the hard way about survival in the **jungle**, and especially how to play the Japanese at their own game. The experience of the campaign was digested by the various planning staffs, and the lessons passed on to the other formations which would be taking on the Japanese all over the southern Pacific.

Realizing the Japanese had landed on Guadalcanal, in July and August the Americans accelerated their plans to retake the island. Commanded by Rear-Admiral Frank Jack Fletcher, whose three aircraft carriers were to provide tactical air support and long-range protection, an expedition was prepared. The commander of the landing forces was Rear-Admiral Richmond K. Turner, and the formation to be landed was Major-

LEFT: *Robert Lawrence Eichelberger was a general officer in the U.S. Army who commanded the Eighth U.S. Army in the South-west Pacific Area during World War II.*

OPPOSITE ABOVE: *Herring (second from left) in Papua with General Douglas MacArthur (center) and Major General Arthur Samuel Allen (right.)*

OPPOSITE BELOW: *Henderson Field on Guadalcanal in late August 1942, soon after Allied aircraft began operating out of the airfield.*

General Alexander A. Vandegrift's 1st Marine Division, reinforced to 19,000 men.

Moving forward from Noumea, in New Caledonia, the 1st Marine Division landed on August 7, the main force coming ashore on Guadalcanal and subsidiary forces on Tulagi and Gavutu, just off the Florida Islands. On these two latter islands, where a seaplane base had been prepared, some 1,500 Japanese were able to put up a spirited defense before being overwhelmed. On Guadalcanal, however, where the marines had landed on the north coast on each side of Lunga Point, opposite the Florida Islands, the 2,200 Japanese quickly dispersed into the jungle, the Americans occupying the airfield area, renamed Henderson Field. As the

OPPOSITE: Hit by bombs from a North American B-25 Mitchell twin-engined medium bomber of the U.S. 5th Army Air Force, a Japanese transport ship sinks.

BELOW: Australian soldiers put on a martial show for the propaganda camera at Port Moresby.

Japanese pondered their reply and gathered their forces, the Americans set about expanding and strengthening their defensive perimeter around Henderson Field.

Meanwhile the invasion fleet, lying between Guadalcanal and the Florida Islands, was coming under intense Japanese air attack from the bases in New Britain. Then, on the following day, the Japanese sprang a major surprise on the Allies in the naval Battle of Savo Island, just off Cape Esperance, up the coast from Lunga Point. Vice-Admiral Shigeyoshi Inoue, commanding the 4th Fleet from Rabaul, sent Vice-Admiral Junichi Mikawa with seven cruisers and a destroyer to attack the Allied

naval forces covering the landings. Arriving off Savo Island on the night of August 8–9, Mikawa encountered a force of one Australian and four U.S. heavy cruisers, commanded by the British Rear-Admiral V.A.C. Crutchley. In a confused night action lasting only 32 minutes, Mikawa's cruisers sank all but one of the Allied cruisers, the last crippled without loss to themselves. Mikawa then retired, although he should have gone on to destroy the Allied transport fleet. He did not know, however, that Fletcher

had pulled his carriers out of the area because of the air threat. One Japanese cruiser, the *Kako*, was sunk by a U.S. submarine on its way back to New Britain. Shocked by his losses, Turner pulled out with all his naval forces, leaving the marines without support. Left much to themselves, apart from air raids, for the next week, the marines continued to consolidate and prepare for the inevitable Japanese attack. On August 18 a regiment, commanded by Colonel Kiyonao Ichiki, landed east of the marine base. Moving overland, Ichiki's force attacked Henderson Field on August 21. The day before, the marines had received their first aircraft, and these played an important part in repulsing this and later attacks. For two days, Ichiki launched a series of determined assaults, all of which were beaten off by the marines. Surprised in the rear by the 1st Marine Division's reserve regiment, Ichiki's force was driven into the sea and was annihilated.

The next day, the U.S. Navy salvaged some of its pride in the Battle of the Eastern Solomons. A force under Rear-Admiral Raizo Tanaka was trying to run some 1,500 reinforcements through to the Japanese defenders of the island,

covered by three aircraft carriers under Vice-Admiral Chuichi Nagumo. The light carrier *Ryujo* was sunk, but the Americans suffered damage to the *Enterprise*, and Tanaka's transport group got through to deliver its troops and bombard the Henderson Field area on the return journey.

On the night of September 7–8 a marine raiding party attacked the Japanese base at Taivu, capturing the plans for the next Japanese attack on Henderson Field. This materialized on September 12 in the form of a series of punches by Major-General Kiyotaki Kawaguchi's 35th Brigade. The fighting raged for two days before the marines finally repulsed the 35th

Brigade, which suffered some 1,200 dead. The action is now remembered as the Battle of Bloody Ridge. Each side was now reinforced: Vandegrift received the 7th Marine and 164th Infantry Regiments, bringing his strength to 23,000, and the Japanese landed the headquarters of the 17th Army and two divisions, being some 20,000 men under Lieutenant-General Harukichi Hyakutake. This reinforcement period lasted until October 22 and was marked on Guadalcanal by intensive skirmishing and patrol activity. It also led to the naval Battle off Cape Esperance during October 11–13, when a cruiser squadron, commanded by Rear-

Admiral Norman Scott, escorting U.S. transports, caught Rear-Admiral Aritomo Goto's cruiser force, also escorting troop transports. Scott's force sank a cruiser and a destroyer and crippled the other two cruisers, but the Japanese landed their troops

ABOVE: *One of the U.S. warships which supported the landing on Guadalcanal in August 1942 was the heavy cruiser Quincy. This was one of three "New Orleans"-class cruisers lost on September 9, 1942 in the Battle of Savo Island.*

OPPOSITE: *Ground crew prepare to load bombs onto a Grumman TBF Avenger attack warplane on Henderson Field, the prize for which the Japanese and Americans fought the Battle of Guadalcanal.*

despite losing two destroyers to land-based bomber attacks afterwards. Between October 13 and 15 two Japanese battleships bombarded Henderson Field, clearly indicating that naval superiority was back in the hands of the Japanese.

During October 23–26, and under the personal command of Lieutenant-General Masao Maruyama, the Japanese then launched a series of furious assaults on Henderson Field, losing some 2,000 men in the process. None of the attacks came near to succeeding. As the Japanese licked their wounds, Vandegrift expanded his perimeter considerably. Had the 1st Marine Division been capable of taking the offensive, there is little doubt that the Japanese would have lost heavily, but the marines were exhausted, and a land stalemate ensued as elements of the 2nd Marine Division began to arrive in the period up to December 8. Activity at sea continued, however, with the Battle of Santa Cruz on October 26–27. Vice-Admiral William L. Halsey had replaced Ghormley, with Rear-Admiral Thomas Kinkaid replacing Fletcher. Kinkaid now met a Japanese carrier force in an action which

The Battle of Guadalcanal

resulted in damage to two Japanese carriers and one American, and also

led to the loss of the U.S. carrier *Hornet*. Although the Japanese had won, it was again only through a great sacrifice of experienced aircrew, a fact that was later to be of great importance.

On Guadalcanal, the exhausted Vandegrift and 1st Marine Division had at last been withdrawn on December 9, their places having been taken by Major-General Alexander M. Patch and the XIV Corps. While Japanese strength hovered at around 20,000, by January 9, 1943 the Americans had 58,000 men of the 2nd Marine, 25th and Americal

Divisions, the last so-named because it had been created from U.S. troops based on New Caledonia.

During the three-phase naval Battle of Guadalcanal during November 12–15, the Americans once again regained command of the sea. In a series of confused battles, the Japanese lost the battleships *Hiei* and *Kirishima*, and the Americans the cruisers *Juneau* and *Northampton*.

Finally, all was ready for the elimination of the Japanese from Guadalcanal. Patch's offensive started on January 10, 1943, and in the next two weeks the Japanese were driven

back from their positions in the jungle west of Henderson Field. By the end of the month, the Japanese 17th Army was penned up in Cape Esperance. From here the destroyers of Tanaka's "Tokyo Express," as usual brilliantly handled, evacuated some 11,000 survivors during February 1–7, leaving the Americans in sole possession of Guadalcanal. The battle had been costly, but the psychological boost to the Allies, following this major victory over the Japanese, was huge.

OPPOSITE: A U.S. Navy destroyer bombards a shore target on January 23, 1943, during the closing stages of the Guadalcanal campaign. This was the time when the last Japanese forces were falling back to Cape Tenaru and their evacuation by the ships of the Tokyo Express.

ABOVE: The U.S. Navy aircraft carrier USS Wasp (CV-7) burning and listing after she was torpedoed by the Japanese submarine I-19, on September 15, 1942, while operating in the south-western Pacific in support of forces on Guadalcanal.

Text-Dependent Questions

1. When did the Battle of Guadalcanal begin?

2. Where is Guadalcanal?

3. Where is Buna and Gona?

Research Projects

Why did American victory at Guadalcanal ensure that Australia was safe from Japanese invasion?

TIME LINE OF WORLD WAR II

1939
Germany invades Poland on September 1.

Two days later Britain and France declare war on Germany.

1940
Rationing starts in the UK.

German "Blitzkrieg" overwhelms and overpowers Belgium, Holland, and France.

Churchill becomes Prime Minister of Britain.

British Expeditionary Force evacuated from Dunkirk.

Britain is victorious in the Battle of Britain. Hitler to postpones invasion plans.

1941
Operation Barbarossa commences – the invasion of Russia begins.

The Blitz continues against Britain. Major cities are badly damaged.

Allies take Tobruk in North Africa, and resist German attacks.

Japan attacks Pearl Harbor, and the U.S. enters the war.

1942
Germany suffers setbacks at Stalingrad and El Alamein.

Singapore falls to the Japanese in February – around 25,000 prisoners taken.

American naval victory at Battle of Midway, in June, marks turning point in Pacific War.

Mass murder of Jewish people at Auschwitz begins.

1943
Germany surrenders at Stalingrad. Germany's first major defeat.

The Allies are victorious in North Africa The invasion of Italy is launched.

Italy surrenders to the Allies, but Germany takes over the fight.

British and Indian forces fight Japanese in Burma.

1944
Allies land at Anzio and bomb monastery at Monte Cassino.

Soviet offensive gathers pace in Eastern Europe.

D-Day: The Allied invasion of France. Paris is liberated in August.

Guam liberated by the U.S. *Okinawa*, and Iwo Jima bombed.

1945
Auschwitz liberated by Soviet troops. Russians reach Berlin. Hitler commits suicide and Germany surrenders on May 7.

Truman becomes President of the U.S. on Roosevelt's death.

Attlee replaces Churchill.

After atomic bombs are dropped on Hiroshima and Nagasaki, Japan surrenders on August 14.

OPPOSITE: A U.S. Marine guards Hill 80 on "Edson's" Ridge, Guadalcanal in 1942. The view is towards the south from whence the Japanese attacked during the battle in September, 1942.

Series Glossary of Key Terms

Allied Powers A coalition of nations that fought against the Axis powers.

ANZAC An Australian or New Zealand soldier.

Appeasement A policy of agreeing to hostile demands in order to maintain peace.

Aryan In Nazi ideology, a Caucasian especially of Nordic type.

Auschwitz An industrial town in Poland and site of Nazi concentration camp during World War II.

Axis Powers An alignment of nations that fought against the Allied forces in World War II.

Blitzkrieg A surprise and violent offensive by air and ground forces.

Concentration camp A camp where prisoners of war are detained or confined.

D-Day June 6, 1944. The Allied invasion of France in World War II began.

Fascism A political movement or philosophy that exalts nation and race above the individual with an autocratic government and a dictator as leader.

Führer A leader or tyrant.

Final Solution The Nazi program to exterminate all the Jews throughout Europe.

Gestapo A secret-police employing devious ways of controlling people considered disloyal.

Holocaust The mass slaughter of European civilians especially the Jews by the Nazis during World War II.

Kamikaze A Japanese pilot trained to make suicidal crash attacks upon ships in World War II.

Lebensraum Territory considered necessary by Nazis for national existence.

Luftwaffe German air force.

Maginot Line Defensive fortifications on the eastern border of France during World War II.

Manhattan Project The code name for the secret U.S. project set up in 1942 to develop an atomic bomb.

Nazi An advocate of policies characteristic of Nazism.

Pact of Steel A military alliance between Nazi Germany and Fascist Italy concluded on May 22, 1939.

Panzer A German tank.

Potsdam Conference A conference held in Potsdam in the summer of 1945 where Roosevelt, Stalin, and Churchill drew up plans for the adminstration of Germany and Poland after World War II ended.

U-boat A German submarine especially in World War I and II.

The Versailles Treaty The treaty imposed on Germany by the Alllied powers in 1920 after the end of World War I.

Yalta Conference A conference held in Yalta in February 1945, where Roosevelt, Stalin, and Churchill planned the finals statge of World War II and agreed to new boundaries and territorial division in Europe.

Further Reading and Internet Resources

WEBSITES

http://www.bbc.co.uk/history/worldwars/wwtwo

http://www.history.com/topics/world-war-ii

https://www.britannica.com/event/World-War-II

http://www.world-war-2.info/

BOOKS

Hourly History. *World War II The Definitive Visual Guide.* Oxford University Press, 2010

Richard Overy. *The New York Times Complete World War II: The Coverage of the Entire Conflict.* 2016

Smithsonian. *World War II The Definitive Visual Guide* DK Publishing Inc., 2015.

If you enjoyed this book take a look at Mason Crest's other war series:

The Civil War, The Vietnam War, Major U.S. Historical Wars.

OPPOSITE: A Japanese freighter in Truk Atoll is hit by a Mark XIII torpedo dropped from a Grumman TBF Avenger of Torpedo Squadron 17 (VT-17) from the aircraft carrier USS Bunker Hill (CV-17), February 17, 1944.

PHOTOGRAPHIC ACKNOWLEDGEMENTS
All images in this book are supplied by Cody Images and are in the public domain.

The content of this book was first published as *WORLD WAR II*.

ABOUT THE AUTHOR
Christopher Chant

Christopher Chant is a successful writer on aviation and modern military matters, and has a substantial number of authoritative titles to his credit. He was born in Cheshire, England in December 1945, and spent his childhood in East Africa, where his father was an officer in the Colonial Service. He returned to the UK for his education at the King's School, Canterbury (1959–64) and at Oriel College, Oxford (1964–68). Aviation in particular and military matters in general have long been a passion, and after taking his degree he moved to London as an assistant editor on the Purnell partworks, *History of the Second World War* (1968–69) and *History of the First World War* (1969–72). On completion of the latter he moved to Orbis Publishing as editor of the partwork, *World War II* (1972–74), on completion of which he decided to become a freelance writer and editor.

Living first in London, then in Lincolnshire after his marriage in 1978, and currently in Sutherland, at the north-western tip of Scotland, he has also contributed as editor and writer to the partworks, *The Illustrated Encyclopedia of Aircraft*, *War Machine*, *Warplane*, *Take-Off*, *World Aircraft Information Files* and *World Weapons*, and to the magazine *World Air Power Journal*. In more recent years he was also involved in the creation of a five-disk CR-ROM series, covering the majority of the world's military aircraft from World War I to the present, and also in the writing of scripts for a number of video cassette and TV programs, latterly for Continuo Creative.

As sole author, Chris has more than 90 books to his credit, many of them produced in multiple editions and co-editions, including more than 50 on aviation subjects. As co-author he has contributed to 15 books, ten of which are also connected with aviation. He has written the historical narrative and technical database for a five-disk *History of Warplanes* CD-ROM series, and has been responsible for numerous video cassette programs on military and aviation matters, writing scripts for several TV programmes and an A–Z 'All the World's Aircraft' section in Aerospace/Bright Star *World Aircraft Information Files* partwork. He has been contributing editor to a number of books on naval, military and aviation subjects as well as to numerous partworks concerned with military history and technology. He has also produced several continuity card sets on aircraft for publishers such as Agostini, Del Prado, Eaglemoss, Edito-Service and Osprey.